the Institute
of Management
F O U N D A T I O N

The Institute of Management (IM) is at the forefront of
management development and best management
practice. The Institute embraces all levels of
management from students to chief executives. It
provides a unique portfolio of services for all
managers, enabling them to develop skills and achieve
management excellence.

For information on the benefits of membership, please
write to:

Department HS
Institute of Management
Cottingham Road
Corby
Northants NN17 1TT

This series is commissioned by the Institute of
Management Foundation.

CONTENTS

■ I N T R O D U C T I O N ■

A basic understanding of finance is very relevant to our personal lives. It is also important to virtually all managers and supervisors, both junior and senior. This has always been so and its significance has increased in recent years.

Changes in the education and health services are high profile examples of its increasing importance in the public sector, and in both the public and private sectors it is necessary for managers to be familiar with financial terms. It is essential that managers understand the financial consequences of the decisions that they make.

All levels of management are regularly confronted with such queries as:

- Is it in the budget?
- Do we have the resources?
- What is the return on investment?
- What do these figures really mean?

Some managers have been financially trained but many more wish to increase their level of understanding. Doing so will enable them to become more effective and improve their scope for development and promotion.

This book is written for managers wishing to achieve this. By setting aside a little time each day for a week you should increase your understanding of the basics of finance.

Please note that your learning on Tuesday and Wednesday will be more effective if you have to hand a company's Annual Report and Accounts. It would be helpful if this could be obtained in advance.

An introduction to Profit Statements

Nearly all private sector businesses are conducted in the hope of making a profit. Surpluses and deficits are also important to large parts of the public sector and to such organisations as charities. An introduction to Profit Statements is therefore very important and an excellent way of starting the week. Today we will work through the following:

The Profit Statement

- A simple example
- A trading company
- A manufacturing company
- Some further concepts expained
- Preparing a full example

A simple example

The heading 'Profit Statement' may be optimistic because it implies that a profit has been made. In some cases it would be more appropriate to call it a Loss Statement.

Profit Statement is the name often given to an internal document setting out the trading activity and results. It is sometimes called the Profit and Loss Account and this is the title normally given in more formal published accounts.

Understanding the principles of a Profit Statement is the first step towards using them to improve future performance. This is covered later in the week but as a first step we will consider a simple example.

Julia Brown writes a book. Her agreement does not provide for royalties, just a fee of £5 000 payable on delivery of the manuscript to the publisher. The costs of the enterprise are small and she pays them in cash as she goes. After receipt of the £5 000 her Profit Statement may well look like the following:

	£	£
Income		5 000
Less costs:		
Typing costs	600	
Stationery	100	
Travel	200	
Postage	30	
Telephone	40	
Miscellaneous	120	
		1 090
Net Profit before Tax		3 910

The profit (or loss) is the difference between money received and all the money paid out. Julia Brown may need the Profit Statement for her bank and for the Inland Revenue. She may use the information herself. For example if she has spent 391 hours working on the book her time has been rewarded at the rate of £10 per hour.

A trading company

Tens of thousands of very small businesses do prepare simple Profit Statements in the manner of the previous example. However, there is another step when things are bought and sold.

It is essential that the costs shown in the Profit Statement relate only to goods sold during the period. All Profit Statements cover a defined period with a specified starting date and a specified closing date. For published accounts this period is often a year but for internal documents it can be whatever period is considered most useful.

Many businesses produce quarterly Profit Statements, but it may be desirable to produce them monthly or even weekly. An intensively managed business such as a major food retailer will produce key profit information on a daily basis. It will withdraw items and change displays according to the results shown.

A distorted result will be given if costs include articles purchased (and paid for) but still in stock at the end of the period. This is overcome by counting stock at the beginning and end of the period. The cost of sales is calculated by adding purchases to the opening stock, then subtracting the closing stock.

If there has been any theft or other form of stock shrinkage the cost of sales will be increased accordingly.

Sometimes the calculation as far as Gross Profit is shown in a separate Trading Account. However, the following simple example shows everything in one Profit Statement.

A Borough Council Leisure Centre operates a bar and prepares monthly Profit Statements. Sales in the month of July were £30 000 and purchases in the same month were £20 000.

Stock of food and drink at June 30th was £10 000 and at July 31st it was £9 000. Wages were £4 000, insurance was £1 500, and the total of all other overheads was £3 000.

The Profit Statement for July was as follows:

	£	£
Sales		30 000
Stock at June 30th	10 000	
Purchases	20 000	
	30 000	
Less stock at July 31st	9 000	
		21 000
Gross Profit		9 000
Less Overheads:		
Wages	4 000	
Insurance	1 500	
All other	3 000	
		8 500
Net Profit		500

A manufacturing company

It is only a small step to set out the Profit Statement of a manufacturing company. It is essential that the cost of manufacturing must exactly relate to the goods sold. The cost of these goods, no more and no less, must be brought into the Profit Statement.

Probably, stocktakes will be necessary at the beginning and end of the period. However, according to circumstances this may not be necessary. If internal controls are good, a calculated stock figure may sometimes be used.

The following example shows the principles. Sometimes the manufacturing costs are shown in a separate Manufacturing Account but in this straightforward example it is included in the Profit Statement.

Chiltern Manufacturing Company Ltd. manufactures and sells household goods. Sales in the year to 31 December 1995 were £750 000. Purchases of raw materials and components in the year were £300 000. Stock at 31 December 1994 was £280 000 and at 31 December 1995 it was £320 000.

Wages of production staff were £200 000, power costs were £60 000 and other production costs were £80 000. Salaries of salesmen, administration staff and management totalled £70 000 and other overheads totalled £85 000.

The Profit Statement for the year to 31 December 1995 is as follows:

	£	£
Sales		750 000
Stock at 31.12.94	280 000	
Purchases	300 000	
	580 000	
Less stock at 31.12.95	320 000	
	260 000	
Production wages	200 000	
Power costs	60 000	
Other production costs	80 000	
Cost of Manufacturing		600 000
		150 000
Less Overheads		
Salaries	70 000	
Other overheads	85 000	
		155 000
Net Loss before Tax		(5 000)

(Note that the brackets indicate a minus figure.)

Key points so far

- There are definite starting and finishing dates
- Total Sales appears near the top
- Profit or Loss appears near the bottom
- Only expenditure on goods actually sold is included

Some further concepts explained

All the examples so far have been extremely simple but
unfortunately real life is often more complicated. It is
necessary to be familiar with certain further principles that
are likely to be incorporated in many Profit Statements.

Accruals (costs not yet entered)
Examples so far have assumed that all costs are paid out as
they are incurred, but this is unrealistic. Invoices are
submitted after the event and some will not have been
entered into the books when they are closed off.

This problem is overcome by adding in an allowance for
these costs. The uninvoiced costs are called accruals.

Let us take as an example a company whose electricity bill is
around £18 000 per quarter. Let us further assume that
accounts are made up to 31 December and that the last
electricity bill was up to 30 November. The accountant will
accrue £6 000 for electricity used but not billed.

If electricity invoices in the period total £60 000 the added
£6 000 will result in £66 000 being shown in the Profit
Statement.

Prepayments (costs entered in advance)
Costs may have been entered into the books for items where
the benefit has not yet been received. An example is an
invoice for production materials delivered after stocktaking.

Consider an insurance premium of £12 000 paid on 1
December for twelve months cover in advance. If the Profit
Statement is made up to 31 December the costs will have

been overstated by $\frac{11}{12}$ × £12 000 = £11 000. The accountant will reduce the costs accordingly. These reductions are called prepayments.

Bad debt reserves and sales ledger reserves
Many businesses sell on credit, and at the end of the period of the Profit Statement money will be owed by customers. Unfortunately not all of this money will necessarily be received. Amongst the possible reasons are:

- Bad debts
- An agreement that customers may deduct a settlement discount if payment is made by a certain date
- The customer may claim that there were shortages, or that he received faulty goods; perhaps goods were supplied on a sale-or-return basis

The prudent accountant will make reserves to cover these eventualities, either a bad debt reserve or sales ledger reserve. Sales (and profit) will be reduced by an appropriate amount.

Time will tell whether the reserves have been fixed at a level that was too high, too low, or just right. If the reserves were too cautious there will be an extra profit to bring into a later Profit Statement. If the reserves were not cautious enough there will be a further cost (and loss) to bring into a later Profit Statement.

Depreciation

Fixed assets are those that will have a useful and productive life longer than the period of the Profit Statement. Examples are factory machinery, computers, motor vehicles and so on.

It would obviously be wrong to charge all the costs of fixed assets to the Profit Statement in the year of purchase. The problem is overcome by charging only a proportion in each year of the expected useful life of the asset.

There are different methods of doing this calculation but the simplest, and most common, is the straight-line method. For example, let us consider an item of equipment costing £300 000 with an expected useful life of five years. The Profit Statement for each year would be charged with £60 000.

This is one of many examples of how profit accounting may differ from the equivalent position in cash. It is quite possible to be profitable and still run out of cash. This will be examined later in the week.

Prudence and the matching of costs to income
Earlier it was explained that costs must be fairly matched to sales. This is so that the costs of the goods actually sold, and only those costs, are brought into the Profit Statement. This is very important, and sometimes very difficult to achieve.

Consider a major building project lasting four years and for which the contractor will be paid £60 000 000. Costs over the four years are expected to be £55 000 000 and the anticipated profit is £5 000 000. Almost certainly the contractor will receive various stage payments over the four years.

This poses a multitude of accounting problems and there is more than one acceptable accounting treatment. The aim must be to bring in both revenue and costs strictly as they are earned and incurred.

The full £60 000 000 will not be credited until the work is complete. In fact there will probably be a retention and it will be necessary to make a reserve for retention work.

Conventions of prudent accounting should ensure that profits are only recognised when they have clearly been earned. Losses on the other hand should be recognised as soon as they can be realistically foreseen.

Before leaving this section, tick off the following boxes to confirm that you understand the principles.

- Accruals are costs incurred, but not yet in the books ☐
- Prepayments are costs in the books, but not yet incurred ☐
- Profit is reduced by expected bad debts ☐
- Depreciation is a book entry to reduce the value of fixed assets ☐
- Profit accounting may differ from cash accounting ☐
- Profit Statements should be prudent ☐
- Costs must be matched to income ☐

Preparing a full example

Sunday is concluded with a slightly more advanced example incorporating the points covered so far. The Profit Statement is set out on page 21.

J. T. Perkins and Son Ltd. manufactures and sells pottery. Sales in the year to 31 December 1995 were £800 000. At 31 December 1995 the company expects to issue a credit note for £10 000 for faulty goods that have been delivered. It also believes that £30 000 owing to it will turn out to be a total bad debt. No such expectations existed at 31 December 1994.

Invoices received for parts and raw materials delivered during the year totalled £240 000, but a £20 000 invoice is awaited for a delivery received on 22 December.

Stock at 31 December 1994 was £308 000. Stock at 31 December 1995 was £302 000.

Manufacturing wages were £150 000 and other manufacturing costs were £60 000. Plant and machinery used for manufacturing originally cost £900 000 and is being depreciated at the rate of 10% per year.

Overheads paid have been

Salaries	*£80 000*
Rent	*£70 000*
Insurance	*£60 000*
Other	*£50 000*

Insurance includes a premium of £7 000 for a year in advance paid on 31 December 1995.

J. T. Perkins and Son Ltd.

Profit Statement for the year to 31 December 1995

	£	£
Sales		790 000
Stock at 31.12.94	308 000	
Add purchases	260 000	
	568 000	
Less stock at 31.12.95	302 000	
	266 000	
Wages	150 000	
Depreciation of plant and machinery	90 000	
Other manufacturing costs	60 000	
Cost of Sales		566 000
Gross Profit		224 000
Less Overheads:		
Salaries	80 000	
Rent	70 000	
Insurance	53 000	
Other	50 000	
Reserve for bad debts	30 000	
		283 000
Net Loss before Tax		(59 000)

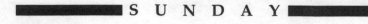

Summary

This Sunday we have been introduced to the basic principles of the following:

- Simple Profit Statements
- Trading companies
- Manufacturing companies
- Accruals and prepayments
- Bad debt reserves and sales ledger reserves
- Depreciation
- Prudence and the matching of costs to income
- An example illustrating most of the principles

Tomorrow, we will take a look at Balance Sheets.

An introduction to Balance Sheets

The main constituents of a set of accounts are the Profit and Loss Account and Balance Sheet. Today, we will study the Balance Sheet and cover the following:

The Balance Sheet
- What is a Balance Sheet?
- Two accounting rules explained
- A simple example
- Some further concepts explained
- Test your knowledge of Balance Sheets

What is a Balance Sheet?

The clue is in the name. A Balance Sheet is a listing of all the balances in the accounting system, and what is more it must balance. The debit balances must equal the credit balances, or put another way the assets must equal the liabilities.

It reveals the overall net worth of the business, although it might be more accurate to say it does so according to sometimes controversial accounting rules. It also gives information about the assets and liabilities.

A freeze-frame picture
Unlike the Profit Statement, the Balance Sheet does not cover a trading period. It is a snapshot of the financial position at a precise moment and the date is always given as part of the heading. It is usually produced to coincide with the last day of the trading period.

To complete the photographic analogy, the Balance Sheet is like a freeze-frame picture of the finances of an enterprise. If the picture were to be taken a day earlier or a day later different financial details would be revealed.

Format of the Balance Sheet
It used to be the custom to set out the figures side by side. The assets (debit balances) went on the right-hand side and the liabilities (credit balances) went on the left-hand side. The two columns of course added up to the same figure.

You may occasionally see a Balance Sheet set out in this form, but it is now much more common to show the figures in a vertical format.

A vertical Balance Sheet shows liabilities deducted from assets in a logical manager. The whole thing adds down to the net worth of the business which is shown at the bottom. The examples in this chapter are produced in the vertical manner.

▰▰▰▰▰ M O N D A Y ▰▰▰▰▰

Grouping of figures

Of course not every individual balance is listed in the
Balance Sheet. If they were, the Balance Sheet of Marks and
Spencer PLC would cover hundreds of pages.

For example a company may have six different bank
accounts, all overdrawn by £100 000. The total of all these
overdrafts would be shown as just one figure of £600 000.

Two accounting rules explained

In order to improve your understanding of Balance Sheets
you must be familiar with the following two fundamental
accounting rules.

- For every debit there must be a credit
- Balance Sheet assets are debit balances and
  Balance Sheet liabilities are credit balances

Debit and credit balances

The first rule of double-entry bookkeeping is that for every debit there must be a credit. This means that an accounting entry always involves one account being debited and another account being credited. Scientists sometimes help themselves remember this by thinking of the law of physics: 'every action has an equal and opposite reaction'.

For example, let us consider what happens when a £10 000 car is purchased. The Motor Vehicles account (which is an asset) is debited with £10 000. The bank account is credited with £10 000. At this stage you might be confused by which entries are debits and which are credits. This is explained in the next section.

Assets and liabilities

Assets in the Balance Sheet are the debit balances in the bookkeeping system. Liabilities in the Balance Sheet are credit balances in the bookkeeping system. This is probably exactly the opposite of what you would expect.

In the Profit Statement, sales and income are the credit balances: costs are the debit balances. The net total of all the balances is the profit or loss.

This one figure goes into the Balance Sheet as a single item. A profit is a credit which is listed with the liabilities. This too is probably exactly the opposite of what you would expect.

The explanation is that the profit belongs to someone outside the business. If the Balance Sheet is for a company, the profit belongs to the shareholders, and one day may be paid to them in the form of a dividend.

A simple example

John Brown commences business as a gardener on July 1st 1995, using the name Cotswold Gardeners. On his first day he pays £6 000 capital into the business. He buys a motor van for £5 000 and a motor mower for £500. They are immediately second-hand so he depreciates them by 20%.

By the end of the gardening season on October 31st he has invoiced his customers £7 000 and been paid in full. His costs have been £2 000, of which he has paid £1 700 and still owes £300.

During the four months he has taken £4 000 out of the business for his living expenses.

Look at the Balance Sheet on the next page and, with a pencil, make sure that you understand how each of the figures is calculated. The figure for profit is after deducting £1 100 depreciation. You should particularly notice that:

- The Balance Sheet is headed and dated, and it balances
- The creditor of £300 is money owing by the business. It is an accrual, which is is one of the things that we studied yesterday
- The business is separate from John Brown's personal affairs. This is why the payment of £4 000 living expenses to John Brown takes money out of the business and affects the Balance Sheet.

John Brown Trading as Cotswold Gardeners
Balance Sheet at October 31st 1995

	£	£
Fixed Assets		
Motor vehicle	4 000	
Motor mower	400	
		4 400
Current Assets		
Bank account	1 800	
Less Current Liabilities		
Creditor	300	
		1 500
		5 900
Capital employed		
Capital paid in at 1/7/95	6 000	
Add profit since 1/7/95	3 900	
	9 900	
Less drawings since 1/7/95	4 000	
		5 900

Some further concepts explained

Balance Sheets that will be audited and published are laid
out according to certain rules and we will look at these
tomorrow. Today, we are concerned with Balance Sheets
prepared just for management use. It will be very helpful if
you are completely familiar with the following concepts.

Fixed assets and depreciation
Fixed assets are grouped together in the Balance Sheet and
one total given for the net value of all of them. Examples of
fixed assets are:

- Freehold property
- Plant and machinery
- Computers
- Motor vehicles

They are assets that will have a value to the business over a
long period, usually understood to be any time longer than
a year.

They do usually lose their value, either with the passage of
time (e.g. a lease) or with use. Therefore, as we have already
seen, they are written off over a number of years. This
depreciation is a book entry and no cash is involved. The
entry is:

- Debit depreciation (thus reducing profit)
- Credit the asset (thus reducing the value of the
  asset)

Current assets
Different types of current asset are listed separately in the
Balance Sheet with one total being shown for the sum of
them all. They are assets with a value available entirely in
the short term, usually understood to be a period less than a
year.

This is either because they are what the business sells, or
because they are money or can quickly be turned into
money. Examples of current assets are:

- Stock
- Money owing by customers (debtors)
- Money in the bank
- Short-term investments

Current liabilities
These too are listed separately in the Balance Sheet with one
total given for the sum of them all. They are liabilities which

the business could be called upon to pay off in the short term, usually within a year. Examples are a bank overdraft and money owing to suppliers (creditors).

Definitions of debtors and creditors

> * A debtor is a person owing money to the business (e.g. a customer for goods delivered)
> * A creditor is a person to whom the business owes money (e.g. an unpaid electricity bill)

Working capital
This is the difference between current assets and current liabilities. In the simple example given earlier it is £1 500.

It is extremely important as we will see later in the week. A business without sufficient working capital cannot pay its debts as they fall due. In this situation it might have to stop trading, even if it is profitable.

Possible alternatives might include raising more capital, taking out a long-term loan, or selling some fixed assets.

Prudent reserves
When something happens that causes an asset to lose value, it is written off. For example, if some stock is stolen, the value of stock in the Balance Sheet is reduced.

The same thing must happen if a prudent view is that an asset has lost some of its value. This happens for example if some of the stock is obsolete and unlikely to sell for full value. Normally the Balance Sheet will just show the reduced value which will be explained with notes.

The creation of a stock reserve reduces the profit. If it is later found that the reserve was not necessary the asset is restored to full value and the profit is increased.

Test your knowledge of Balance Sheets

A working Balance Sheet is given on the next page. For the sake of brevity, taxation and the explanatory notes have been omitted.

Now test your knowledge of Balance Sheets by answering the following questions. The answers are given at the top of today's last page but you should write down your own answers before checking.

1 Is the capital employed of £448 000 an asset or a liability?

2 Suggest two possible additional types of current asset.

3 What is the working capital?

4 What would the working capital be if stock valued at £10 000 was sold for £18 000 (payable after 30 days) and if an extra piece of machinery was purchased for £30 000?

5 Assume that a customer had paid a debt of £3 000 written off as bad at October 31st 1994.

   a What would the profit for the year have been?

   b What would be Trade Debtors at October 31st 1995?

Patel Brothers

Balance Sheet at October 31st 1995

	£	£
Fixed Assets		
Freehold premises	200 000	
Fixtures and fittings	30 000	
Plant and machinery	50 000	
		280 000
Current Assets		
Stock	130 000	
Trade debtors	190 000	
Other debtors	16 000	
	336 000	
Less Current Liabilities		
Trade creditors	70 000	
Bank overdraft	48 000	
	118 000	
		218 000
Bank Loan repayable on 31/12/98		(50 000)
		448 000
Capital employed		
Capital at 31/10/94	350 000	
Add profit for year	300 000	
	650 000	
Less drawings for year	202 000	
		448 000

Answers

1 Liability

2 Short-term investments, bank accounts, cash

3 £218 000

4 £196 000

5 **a** £303 000

   b £190 000 (no change)

Summary

This Monday we have been introduced to the basic principles of the following:

- What is a Balance Sheet?
- Format of the Balance Sheet
- Elementary rules of double entry bookkeeping
- An example of a simple Balance Sheet
- Fixed assets and depreciation
- Current assets and current liabilities
- Debtors and creditors
- Working capital
- Prudent reserves

Finally, we have examined another Balance Sheet and tested our understanding of it.

Tomorrow, we will try to understand published accounts.

Understanding published accounts

Today, we will be studying published accounts and it will
be helpful if you obtain a set of accounts. The accounts will
be particularly useful if they are for a company well known
to you, such as your employer. Advice on how to get hold of
published accounts is given in the first section of today's
work.

Today's programme is:

- Availability of published accounts
- What is included
- Profit and Loss Account and Balance Sheet
- The remainder of the Annual Report and Accounts

Availability of published accounts

Accounts are published for one or both of the following
reasons:

- Because it is required by law
- As a public relations exercise

All companies are required by law to produce accounts annually although, subject to strict limits, the period can be changed. They must then file them at Companies House. A private company must file within 10 months of the Balance Sheet date at the end of the accounting period and a public company must file within seven months. The law, and accepted accountancy practice, stipulate the minimum contents and standards of the accounts. Companies can, and often do, include more than this required minimum.

Certain bodies other than companies are also required to produce accounts. Examples are building societies, charities and local authorities. Our work today deals exclusively with the accounts of companies.

Companies House
Accounts must be filed at Companies House and are available for inspection by shareholders, creditors, staff or anyone at all. It may sound like a charter for nosy parkers, but it is the price shareholders pay for the privilege of limited liability.

The address for companies registered in England and Wales is *The Registrar of Companies, Companies House, Cardiff CF4 3UZ*. In December 1995 there were 1 200 593 live companies on the register. Companies registered in Scotland, Northern Ireland, Jersey etc. are registered at different offices.

How to obtain published accounts

A public company will probably be willing to make accounts available. A request should be made to the Company Secretary or the Public Relations department.

Alternatively you can get the accounts of any company, even the corner shop, by applying to Companies House. This can be done at Cardiff or at one of their offices around the country. This can be done in person but for a modest fee an agent will do it for you.

Late filing

Unfortunately, a significant minority of companies file their accounts late or even not at all. This is an offence for which the directors can be punished, but accounts are still sometimes filed late.

What is included

Have a close look at the Annual Report and Accounts that you have obtained. You will certainly find the following:

- Directors' Report
- Auditor's Report
- Profit and Loss Account and Balance Sheet
- Source and Applications of Funds Statement
- Consolidated accounts (if it is a holding company)
- Explanatory notes

You will certainly find all these because they are required by law and good accountancy practice. You may also find a summary of the key figures over a number of years which can be very useful. Not surprisingly this may be more likely to be present if it reveals a steadily improving position.

You may well also find a Chairman's report. This may be very useful or it may not. It will almost certainly have been written with public relations in mind, but may well contain a lot of interesting information about the company's position, policies and objectives. It is by no means unknown for the chairman to include his personal views about the state of the world and the deficiencies of the government. You probably already have your own views on these matters.

You should note that very small companies are permitted to file summarised information.

At this point it is a good idea to test your ability to find information in your Annual Report and Accounts. Can you answer the following questions? The most likely places to find the answers are shown on the next page.

1   What is the pre-tax profit?

2 Do the auditors have any reservations?

3 What is the working capital (net current assets)?

4 What were the total exports?

5 Did the company make any political or charitable contributions?

6 What was the total amount paid out in wages and salaries?

7 Was there a net cash outflow in the period?

Where to find the answers
1 Profit and Loss Account

2 Auditor's Report

3 Balance Sheet (this was examined yesterday)

4 Notes

5 Directors' Report

6 Notes

7 Source and Application of Funds Statement

Profit and Loss Account and Balance Sheet

These are the core of the accounts and we have already looked at some of the principles on Sunday and Monday. The Profit and Loss Account will give the figures for the previous period as well as the current period. Figures in the Balance Sheet will be given as at the previous Balance Sheet date as well as for the present one.

Now we will have a look at what will be shown in the published Profit and Loss Account and Balance Sheet of a company. Some of the information may be given in notes with a suitable cross-reference.

Profit and Loss Account
Most people consider that the key figure is the one for Profit before Tax. You may think that taxation is fair, or at any rate inevitable, and that Profit before Tax is the best measure of the company's success. The bottom part of the Profit and Loss Account will look rather like this. Fictitious figures have been inserted.

Profit before Tax	£10 000 000
Less Tax on Profit	£3 200 000
Profit for the Year	£6 800 000
Less Dividends Paid and Proposed	£4 000 000
Retained Profit for the Year	£2 800 000
Retained Profit brought forward	£7 000 000
Retained Profit carried forward	£9 800 000

In this example Her Majesty's Government is taking £3 200 000 of the profit and £4 000 000 is being distributed to shareholders. The company started the current period with undistributed profits of £7 000 000 and it is prudently adding £2 800 000 to this figure. Undistributed Profits are now £9 800 000 and this figure will appear in the Balance Sheet.

The Profit and Loss Account will give the turnover which is the total invoiced sales in the period. This is very important and it is useful to work out the relationship between the profit and the turnover.

Balance Sheet
Fixed assets is normally the first item appearing in the Balance Sheet. Usually you will see just one figure for the net amount of the fixed assets and a cross-reference to a note. This note will:

a   break down the assets by type
b   give cumulative expenditure for each type
c   give cumulative depreciation for each type
d   give net asset value for each type (B minus C)
e   state the depreciation policy for each type

The fixed assets are usually one of the most interesting sections of the accounts. This is because it is rare for the assets to be worth exactly the figure shown.

Depreciation according to accounting rules rarely reflects the real-life situation, especially in times of inflation. One wonders what would be the book value of St. Pauls Cathedral if the Church of England had followed depreciation rules at the time of Sir Christopher Wren.

In practice, companies sometimes revalue property assets thought not usually other assets. Asset strippers specialise in buying undervalued companies then selling the fixed assets for more than book value. This is one reason why the details are so important.

Current assets and current liabilities First the current assets will be listed by type and a total of the current assets will be given. Then the current liabilities will be listed by type and the total of the current liabilities will be given.

The difference between the two figures will be stated and this is the *net current assets* or the *working capital*. A problem is usually indicated if the current assets are smaller than the current liabilities or only slightly larger.

The assets and liabilities will be cross-referenced to notes giving appropriate details such as the following:

- A breakdown of stocks into finished goods and work in progress
- A split of debtors between trade debtors (customers) and other debtors
- Details of the different types of creditors

Capital and reserves On Monday we examined the net worth of an organisation shown at the bottom of its Balance Sheet. This section is the net worth of the company.

If the company were to be wound up, and in the unlikely event of all the assets and liabilities being worth exactly book value, the total of this section is the amount that would be distributed to shareholders.

A note will give details of the different types of share capital if there are more than one. It will also give the figures for the different types of reserves, and the retained figure in the Profit and Loss Account.

The remainder of the Annual Report and Accounts

The Directors' Report
The directors are required by law to provide certain information. This includes, for example, the amount of exports and details of any political or charitable contributions. This information is usually disclosed in the Directors' Report.

Notes to the Accounts
There are always notes to the Profit and Loss Account and Balance Sheet. Their purpose is to give further details, and they are in the form of notes to prevent the accounts getting horribly detailed and complicated. Many of the notes give a breakdown of such figures as stock and debtors.

The notes also state the accounting policies and conventions used in the preparation of the accounts. These are extremely important because these policies can greatly affect the figures. An example of such a policy would be to value stocks at the lower of cost and net realiseable value. Any change to this policy could greatly affect the profit figure.

Source and Applications of Funds Statement
There are sometimes disputes about the figures in the Profit
and Loss Account and Balance Sheet. This is one reason why
cash is so important. Cash is much more a matter of fact
rather than of opinion. It is either there or it is not there.

Where the cash came from (banks, shareholders, customers)
is also a matter of fact. So too is where the cash went to
(dividends, wages, suppliers, etc.). The statement gives all
this information.

The Auditor's Report
The law requires company accounts to be audited by a
person or firm holding one of the approved qualifications.
No audit is required if annual turnover is less than £90 000
and a compilation report instead of an audit is required if
annual turnover is between £90 000 and £350 000. The
auditors will state whether in their opinion the accounts
give a true and fair view.

If the auditors have reservations, they will give reasons for
their concern.

Serious qualifications are rare, partly because it is in the interests of directors that they be avoided. Technical, and less serious, qualifications are more common. It is a matter of judgement how seriously each one is regarded.

Consolidated Accounts
A large group may have a hundred or more companies. It would obviously give an incomplete picture if each of these companies gave information just about its own activities. This is especially true when companies in a group trade with each other.

This is why the holding company must include consolidated accounts as well as its own figures. The effect of inter-group trading is eliminated in the consolidated accounts. This does not, however, remove the obligation for every company in the group to prepare and file its own accounts.

Summary

Today we have:

- Examined the obligation to publish accounts and seen where copies can be obtained
- Seen what is included in the Annual Report and Accounts
- Tested our knowledge
- Conducted an outline study of each section of the Annual Report and Accounts

Tomorrow, we will go on to look at accounting ratios and investment decisions.

Accounting ratios and investment decisions

So far we have studied accounts and what they mean. Now we will devote a day to the active use of financial information. First we shall take a look at ratios in the accounts, and then move on to investment decisions.

Today's programme is:

- Accounting ratios
- Four key questions
- Testing our understanding of accounting ratios
- Investment decisions

Accounting ratios

There are many useful ratios that can be taken from accounts. The following are among the most important but there are many others. It is a good idea to have a set of accounts with you as you work through this section. Pick out relevant figures, work out the ratios, and try to draw conclusions.

Profit and turnover
For example:

Annual turnover	£10 000 000
Annual profit before tax	£1 000 000
Profit to turnover	10%

This uses Profit before Tax but it may be more useful to use Profit after Tax. Perhaps you want to define profit as excluding the charge for bank interest. You should select the definition most relevant to your circumstances. The ratio may be expressed in different ways (e.g. 1 to 10 instead of 10%).

Return on capital employed
For example:

Capital employed	£5 000 000
Annual profit before tax	£1 000 000
Return on capital employed	20%

Again the profit may be expressed before or after tax.

Capital employed is the net amount invested in the business by the owners and is taken from the Balance Sheet. Many people consider this the most important ratio of all. It is useful to compare the result with a return that can be obtained outside the business. If a Building Society is paying a higher rate perhaps the business should be closed down and the money put in the Building Society.

Note that there are two ways of improving the return. In the example, the return on capital employed would be 25% if the profit was increased to £1 250 000. It would also be 25% if the capital employed was reduced to £4 000 000.

Stock turn
For example:

Annual turnover	£10 000 000
Annual cost of sales (60%)	£6 000 000
Stock value	£1 500 000
Stock turn	4

As the name implies this measures the number of times that total stock is used (turned over) in the course of a year. The higher the stock turn the more efficiently the business is being run.

It is important that the terms are completely understood and that there are no abnormal factors. Normally the definition of stock includes all finished goods, work in progress, and raw materials.

The stock value will usually be taken from the closing Balance Sheet but you need to consider if this is a typical figure. If the business is seasonal it may not be. A better results may be obtained if the average of several stock figures throughout the year can be used.

Number of days credit granted
For example:

Annual turnover	£10 000 000
Trade debtors	£1 500 000
Number of days credit	55

The calculation is $\dfrac{1\ 500\ 000}{10\ 000\ 000} \times 365 = 55$ days

Obviously the lower the number of days the more efficiently the business is being run. The figure for trade debtors normally comes from the closing Balance Sheet and care must be taken. If £1 500 000 of the £10 000 000 turnover came in the final month then the number of days credit is really 31 instead of 55.

Number of days credit taken
The principle of the calculation is exactly the same. In this case the figure for closing trade creditors is compared with that for the annual purchases.

If you have access to frequently produced management accounts the ratios will be more useful.

Before leaving accounting ratios please take warning from a true story. Some years ago one of the accountancy bodies

asked examination candidates to work with ratios and draw
conclusions from a Balance Sheet given in the examination
paper.

Many of the students said that the company was desperately
short of working capital and predicted imminent trouble.
One hopes that they were mistaken because the Balance
Sheet had been taken from the latest published accounts of
Marks and Spencer. The students had overlooked the fact
that nearly all sales were for cash and that the business was
well managed.

Four key questions

There are many traps in using financial information and
interpreting accounting ratios. You are advised to approach
the job with caution and always to keep in mind four key
questions.

Am I comparing like with like?
Financial analysts pay great attention to the notes in
accounts and to stated accounting policies. One of the

reasons for this is that changes in accounting policies can affect the figures and hence the comparisons.

Consider a company that writes off research and development costs as overheads as soon as they are incurred. Then suppose that it changes policy and decides to capitalise the research and development, holding it in the Balance Sheet as having a long-term value. A case can be made for either treatment but the change makes it difficult to compare ratios for different years.

Is there an explanation?
Do not forget that there may be a special reason for an odd-looking ratio.

For example, greetings card manufacturers commonly deliver Christmas cards in August with an arrangement that payment is due on January 1st. The June 30th Balance Sheet may show that customers are taking an average of 55 days credit. The December 31st Balance Sheet may show that customers are taking an average of 120 days credit.

This does not mean that the position has deteriorated dreadfully and the company is in trouble. The change in the period of credit is an accepted feature of the trade and happens every year. It is of course important, particularly as extra working capital has to be found at the end of each year.

What am I comparing it with?
A ratio by itself only has a limited value. It needs to be compared with something. Useful comparisons may be with the company budget, last year's ratio, or competitors' ratios.

Do I believe the figures?

You may be working with audited and published figures. On the other hand you may only have unchecked data rushed from the accountant's desk. This sort of information may be more valuable because it is up to date. But beware of errors. Even if you are not a financial expert, if it feels wrong, perhaps it is wrong.

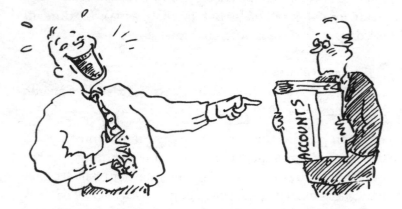

Test your understanding of accounting ratios

The Balance Sheet of Bristol Adhesives Ltd. appears on the next page. The following information is available for the year to October 31st 1995.

Turnover was	£6 600 000
Profit before Tax was	£66 000
The bank overdraft limit is	£800 000
Cost of sales was	50%

1 What was the ratio of Profit to Turnover? ....

2 What was the Return on Capital Employed? ....

3 What was the Stock Turn?   ....

4 What was the number of days credit granted?   ....

5 **a** What is the working capital?   ....

   b Does this give cause for concern?   ....

Answers are given on the last page of today's work.

Bristol Adhesives Ltd.

Balance Sheet at October 31st 1995

	£	£
Fixed Assets		2 000 000
Current Assets		
Stock	1 800 000	
Trade debtors	700 000	
Other debtors	300 000	
	2 800 000	
Less Current Liabilities		
Trade creditors	1 400 000	
Bank overdraft	800 000	
Other creditors	400 000	
	2 600 000	
Net Current Assets		200 000
		2 200 000
Capital and Reserves		
Called-up share capital		1 500 000
Profit and Loss Account		700 000
		2 200 000

Investment decisions

Some investment decisions are easy to make. Perhaps a government safety regulation makes an item of capital expenditure compulsory. Or perhaps an essential piece of machinery breaks down and just has to be replaced.

Many other investment descisions are not nearly so clear cut and hinge on whether the proposed expenditure will generate sufficient future cash savings to justify itself. There are many very sophisticated techniques for aiding this decision, but today we will look at three techniques that are commonly used.

Payback
This has the merit of being extremely simple to calculate and understand. It is a simple measure of the period of time taken for the savings made to equal the capital expenditure. For example:

A new machine will cost £100 000. It will save £40 000 running expenses in the first year and £30 000 per year after that.

The payback period would be three years because this is the time taken for the saving on costs to equal the original expenditure. Hopefully this only took you a few seconds to work out and it is very useful information to have.

The disadvantage of the payback technique is that no account is given to the value of holding money. The £30 000 saved in year three is given equal value to £30 000 of the £100 000 paid out on day one. In fact, inflation and loss of interest mean that, in reality, it is less valuable.

Return on investment

This takes the average of the money saved over the life of the asset and expresses it as a percentage of the original sum invested. For example:

A new machine will cost £100 000 and have a life of eight years. It will save £40 000 running expenses in the first year, and £30 000 in each of the remaining seven years.

The return on investment is $\dfrac{250\,000 \times 100}{100\,000 \times 8} = 31.25\%$ p.a.

Return on investment, like payback, takes no account of the time factor. A pound in eight years' time is given equal value with a pound today.

Discounted cash flow

This technique takes account of the fact that money paid or received in the future is not as valuable as money paid or received now. For this reason it is considered superior to payback and to return on investment. However, it is not so simple to calculate and understand.

There are variations to the discounted cash flow technique but the principles are illustrated by the following example.

The purchase of two competing pieces of machinery are under consideration. Machine A costs £100 000 and will save £60 000 in year 1 and £55 000 in year 2. Machine B costs £90 000 and will save £55 000 in both year 1 and year 2. The savings are taken to occur at the end of each year and the company believes that the money saved will earn 10% p.a. in bank interest.

The calculations are:

	Machine A	Machine B
Expenditure now	£100 000	£90 000
Less year 1 savings (discounted)	£54 600	£50 050
	£45 400	£39 950
Less year 2 savings (discounted)	£45 650	£45 650
Savings at Net Present Value	£250	£5 700

The example has of course been unrealistically simplified. However, it shows that after bringing the future values back to Net Present Value, Machinery B is the better purchase.

Answers to questions on pp. 52–3.

1 $\dfrac{66\,000}{6\,600\,000} = 1\%$

2 $\dfrac{66\,000}{2\,200\,000} = 3\%$

3 $\dfrac{3\,300\,000}{1\,800\,000} = 1.8$

4 $\dfrac{700\,000}{6\,600\,000} \times 365 = 39$ days

5 a) £200 000

   b) Yes (cause for further enquiry anyway)

Summary

Today, we have looked at how financial information is actively used and specifically at:

- Useful accounting ratios
- Four possible reasons for caution
- Our understanding of accounting ratios
- Financial techniques aiding investment decisions

Tomorrow, we shall go on to increase our understanding of cash and the management of working capital.

Cash and the management of working capital

It is sometimes said that cash is king and today we look at the importance and management of cash. We also look at the management of working capital and the place of cash within it. The programme is:

- The distinctions between profit and cash
- What is cash?
- The Cash-Flow Forecast
- The management of working capital

The distinctions between profit and cash

Cash is completely different to profit, a fact which is not always properly appreciated. It is possible, and indeed quite common, for a business to be profitable but short of cash. Among the differences are the following:

- Money may be collected from customers more slowly (or more quickly) than money is paid to suppliers.
- Capital expenditure (unless financed by hire purchase or similar means) has an immediate impact on cash. The effect on profit, by means of depreciation, is spread over a number of years.
- Taxation, dividends and other payments to owners are an appropriation of profit. Money is taken out of the business, which may be more or less than the profit.
- An expanding business will have to spend money on materials, items for sale, wages, etc., before it completes the extra sales and gets paid. Purchases and expenses come first. Sales and profit come later.

It is worth illustrating the problems of an expanding business with a hypothetical but realistic example.

Company A manufactures pens. It has a regular monthly turnover of £20 000. The cost of the pens is £10 000 (50%). Other monthly costs are £8 000 and its monthly profit is £2 000.

At December 31st, Company A has £3 000 in the bank and is owed £40 000 by customers to whom it allows two months' credit. It owes £15 000 to suppliers who are paid within 30 days. £3 000 of the monthly costs are payable in cash.

The company secures an additional order for £60 000. The extra pens will take two months to make and will be delivered on February 28th. The customer will then have 60 days to pay.

The cost of the additional pens will be £30 000 (50%) and there will be extra expenses of £14 000 in the two months. The new order will contribute a very satisfactory £16 000 extra profit.

By April 30th, Company A will have made £24 000 profit. This is the regular £2 000 a month plus the £16 000 from the additional order.

Now let us assume that the new customer pays on May 1st, just one day late. Despite the extra profit, on April 30th the £3 000 bank balance will have turned into a £33 000 overdraft. The calculation is as follows:

Balance at December 31st	£3 000
Add receipts in four months	£80 000
	£83 000
Less payments to creditors in four months	£90 000
	(£7 000)
Less cash expenses in four months	£26 000
Overdraft at April 30th	(£33 000)

What is cash?

Cash includes the notes and coins in the petty cash box. It also includes money in bank current accounts, and money in various short-term investment accounts that can quickly be turned into available cash.

It is common for a Balance Sheet to show only a tiny amount for cash. This is because the business has an overdraft and only such things as the petty cash are included.

Practical management usage of the term cash includes a negative figure for an overdraft. A Cash-Flow Forecast can result in a series of forecast overdrafts.

The Cash-Flow Forecast

It is extremely important that cash receipts and payments are effectively planned and anticipated. Only if this is done is it possible to ensure that sufficient resources are available and that the money does not run out. A good manager will also plan so that not too many resources are tied up.

This can be done in isolation but it is better done as part of the overall budgeting process. Budgets are examined on Saturday.

The preparation of a detailed Cash-Flow Forecast will yield many benefits. Calculating and writing down the figures may suggest ideas as to how they can be improved. For example, the figures for cash payments from trade debtors will be based on an estimate of the average number of days' credit that will be taken. This will pose the question of whether or not payments can be speeded up.

When the Cash-Flow Forecast is finished it will be necessary to consider if the results are acceptable. Even if resources are available the results might not be satisfactory, and improvements will have to be worked out.

If sufficient resources are not available, either changes must be made or extra resources arranged. Perhaps an additional bank overdraft can be negotiated. Either way, a well-planned document will help managers to take action in good time.

The principles of a Cash-Flow Forecast are best illustrated with an example and a good one is given on the next page.

Variations in the layout are possible but a constant feature should be the running cash or overdraft balance.

Do not overlook contingencies and do not overlook the possibility of a peak figure within a period. For example Ace Toys Ltd. are forecast to have £17 000 on March 31st and £5 000 on April 30th. Both forecasts could be exactly right and the company still need a £15 000 overdraft on April 15th.

Ace Toys Ltd. – Cash-Flow Forecast for half year

	January £000	February £000	March £000	April £000	May £000	June £000
Receipts						
UK customers	50	55	55	55	60	80
Export customers	20	20	20	20	25	20
All other	5	5	8	2	12	6
	75	80	83	77	97	106
Payments						
Purchase ledger suppliers	30	33	29	40	44	38
Wages (net)	14	13	13	17	13	13
PAYE and National Insurance	4	4	4	4	5	4
Corporation tax	–	–	30	–	–	–
Capital expenditure	7	4	25	20	2	2
All other	8	9	9	8	6	11
	63	63	110	89	70	68
Excess of Receipts over Payments	12	17	(27)	(12)	27	38
Add Opening Bank Balance	15	27	44	17	5	32
Closing Bank Balance	27	44	17	5	32	70

It will help fix the principles in your mind if you now prepare your own personal Cash-Flow Forecast. Use the form below.

The figures will be smaller but the principles are identical. The opening bank balance in month one should be the latest figure on your personal bank statement.

	Month 1	Month 2	Month 3
	£	£	£
Receipts			
Salary			
Interest			
Dividends			
Other (specify)			
	_____	_____	_____
	_____	_____	_____
Payments			
Mortgage or rent			
Telephone			
Gas and electricity			
Food			
Car expenses			
Other (specify)			
	_____	_____	_____
	_____	_____	_____
Excess of receipts over Payments			
Add Opening Bank Balance			
Closing Bank Balance	_____	_____	_____
	_____	_____	_____

The management of working capital

Is it important?
The effective management of working capital can be critical
to the survival of the business. It is hard to think of anything
more important than that. Many businesses that fail are
profitable at the time of their failure. The reason for the
failure is a shortage of working capital.

Furthermore, effective management of working capital is
likely to improve profitability significantly. Turn back to
Wednesday's section on return on capital employed. You
will remember that the percentage return increases as
capital employed is reduced. Effective management of
working capital can reduce the capital employed. It
increases profits as well as enabling managers to sleep
soundly without worries.

The four largest elements affecting working capital are
usually debtors, stock, creditors and cash. Success in
managing the first three affect cash, which can be reinvested
in the business or distributed. We will consider the three
elements in turn.

Debtors
British business is plagued by slow payment of invoices.
Various studies show that a typical invoice with a nominal
30 day settlement period is on average paid after about 78
days. This is catastrophic and an improvement can
significantly affect working capital.

It is a great problem for managers, who sometimes are
frightened of upsetting customers and feel that there is little
that they can do. This is completely the wrong attitude.

Customer relations must always be considered, but a great deal can be done. Some practical steps are summarised in the box below:

Practical steps for credit control

- Have the right attitude; ask early and ask often
- Make sure that payment terms are agreed in advance
- Do not underestimate the strength of your position
- Give credit control realistic status and priority
- Have well-thought-out credit policies
- Concentrate on the biggest and most worrying debts first
- Be efficient; send out invoices and statements promptly
- Deal with queries quickly and efficiently
- Make full use of the telephone, your best aid
- Use legal action if necessary

This may sound obvious, but it usually works. To sum up: **be efficient, ask and be tough if necessary.**

Stock
The aim should be to keep stock as low as is realistically feasible, and to achieve as high a rate of stock turnover as is realistically feasible. In practice, it is necessary to compromise between the wish to have stock as low as possible, and the need to keep production and sales going with a reasonable margin of safety.

Exactly how the compromise is struck will vary from case to case. Purchasing and production control are highly skilled functions and great effort may be expended getting it right.

You may be familiar with the phrase 'just in time deliveries'. This is the technique of arranging deliveries of supplies frequently and in small quantities. In fact, just in time to keep production going. It is particularly successful in Japan where, for example, car manufacturers keep some parts for production measured only in hours.

It is not easy to achieve and suppliers would probably like to make large deliveries at irregular intervals. It may pay to approach the problem with an attitude of partnership with key suppliers, and to reward them with fair prices and continuity of business.

Finished goods should be sold, delivered, and invoiced as quickly as possible.

Creditors

It is not ethical advice, but there is an obvious advantage in paying suppliers as slowly as possible. Many firms do adopt this policy, and in particular large and strong companies often impose it on small and weak suppliers.

Slow payment does not affect the net balance of working capital, but it does mean that both cash and creditors are higher than would otherwise be the case. Apart from moral considerations there are some definite disadvantages in a policy of slow payment:

- Suppliers will try and compensate with higher prices or lower service
- Best long-term results are often obtained by fostering mutual loyalty with key suppliers; it pays to consider their interests
- If payments are already slow, there will be less scope for taking longer to pay in response to a crisis

For these reasons it is probably not wise to adopt a consistent policy of slow payment, at least with the important suppliers. It is better to be hard but fair, and to ensure that this fair play is rewarded with keen prices, good service, and perhaps prompt payment discounts.

There may be scope for timing deliveries to take advantage of payment terms. For example if the terms are 'net monthly account', a June 30th delivery will be due for payment on July 31st. A July 1st delivery will be due for payment on August 31st.

Summary

Today we have:

- Studied the distinctions between profit and cash
- Examined an example illustrating the differences
- Seen what is meant by the term 'cash'
- Looked at Cash-Flow Forecasts
- Studied the importance of working capital and looked closely at debtors, stock, and creditors

Tomorrow, we will continue by taking a look at costing.

Costing

A basic understanding of the principles of costing is
important in business management. The aim today is to
master these key basic principles.

Costing principles

- The value of costing
- The uses of costing
- Absorption costing
- Break even charts
- Marginal costing and standard costing

↖ HIDDEN COST!

The value of costing

The value of cost accounts can be illustrated with a simple
example. Consider a company with three products. Its
financial accounts show sales of £1 000 000, total costs of
£700 000, and a profit of £300 000. The managers think that

this is very good and that no significant changes are necessary. However, the cost accounts disclose the following:

	Product 1 £000	Product 2 £000	Product 3 £000	Total £000
Sales	600	300	100	1 000
Fixed costs	70	60	50	180
Variable costs	280	160	80	520
Total costs	350	220	130	700
Profit Contribution	250	80	(30)	300

This shows that Product 1, as well as having the biggest proportion of sales, is contributing proportionately the most profit. Despite the overall good profit, Product 3 is making a negative contribution.

The obvious reaction might be to discontinue Product 3, but this may well be a mistake. £50 000 of fixed costs would have to be allocated to the other two products and the total profit would be reduced to £280 000.

Product 3 should probably only be discontinued if the fixed costs can be cut, or if the other two products can be expanded to absorb the £50 000 fixed costs.

Financial accounts provide historical financial information to enable the organisation to comply with the law. They also, of course, do more than this and provide useful financial information for managers.

Cost accounts go further than the financial accounts and break down costs to individual products and cost centres.

Much, but not all, of the information comes from the financial accounts and it is important that cost accounts are reconciled with them.

Cost accounts are much more valuable if the information can be made speedily available. Sometimes it is necessary to compromise between speed and accuracy.

The uses of costing

It costs time and money to produce costing information and it is only worth doing if the information is put to good use. The following are some of these uses.

To control costs
Possession of detailed information about costs is of obvious value in the controlling of those costs.

To promote responsibility
Management theorists agree that power and responsibility should go together. Timely and accurate costing information will help top management hold all levels of management responsible for the budgets that they control.

Care should be taken that managers are not held responsible for costs that are not within their control. As many readers will know from bitter experience, this does sometimes happen.

To aid business decisions
The case given earlier today might be such a decision. Management must decide what to do about the unprofitable product.

To aid decisions on pricing
We live in competitive times and the old 'cost plus' contracts are now very rarely encountered. What the market will bear is usually the main factor in setting prices. Nevertheless, detailed knowledge concerning costs is an important factor in determining prices. Only in exceptional circumstances will managers agree to price goods at below cost, and they will seek to make an acceptable margin over cost.

Accurate costing is vital when tenders are submitted for major contracts and errors can have significant consequences. Topical instances are the Channel Tunnel and certain defence contracts.

Absorption costing

This takes account of all costs and allocates them to individual products or cost centres. Some costs relate directly to a product and this is quite straightforward in principle, although very detailed record keeping may be necessary. Other costs do not relate to just one product and these must be allocated according to a fair formula. These indirect costs must be *absorbed* by each product.

There is not a single correct method of allocating overhead costs to individual products and it is sometimes right to allocate different costs in different ways. The aim should be to achieve fairness in each individual case.

Among the costs that can be entirely allocated to individual products are direct wages and associated employment costs, materials, and bought-in components.

Among the costs that cannot be entirely allocated to individual products are indirect wages (cleaners, maintenance staff, etc.), wages of staff such as salesmen and accountants, and general overheads such as rent and rates.

Great care must be taken in deciding the best way to allocate the non-direct costs. There are many different ways and the following two are common examples.

Production hours
The overhead costs are apportioned according to the direct production hours charged to each product or cost centre. For example, consider a company with just two products, A having 5 000 hours charged and B having 10 000 hours

charged. If the overhead is £60 000, product A will absorb
£20 000 and product B will absorb £40 000.

Machine hours
The principle is the same but the overhead is allocated
according to the number of hours that the machinery has
been running.

This is best illustrated with an example. You should try to
write down the cost statement before checking the solution.

*Fruit Products Ltd. manufactures three types of jam. Its overhead
costs in January are £18 000 and it allocates them in the
proportion of direct labour costs. The following details are
available for January.*

	Strawberry	Raspberry	Apricot	Total
Jars manufactured	26 000	60 000	87 000	173 000
Direct labour	£2 000	£4 000	£6 000	£12 000
Ingredients	£6 000	£11 000	£17 000	£34 000
Other direct costs	£2 000	£3 000	£6 000	£11 000

The resulting cost statement is shown overleaf:

Jam costs

Fruit Products Ltd. – January Cost Statement

	Strawberry	Raspberry	Apricot	Total
Jars produced	26 000	60 000	87 000	173 000
	£	£	£	£
Costs				
Direct labour	2 000	4 000	6 000	12 000
Ingredients	6 000	11 000	17 000	34 000
Other direct costs	2 000	3 000	6 000	11 000
Total Direct Costs	10 000	18 000	29 000	57 000
Overhead allocation	3 000	6 000	9 000	18 000
Total Cost	13 000	24 000	38 000	75 000
Cost per Jar	50.0p	40.0p	43.7p	43.4p

You will notice that in the example, direct labour is smaller than the overhead cost that is being allocated. If the overheads had been allocated in a different way, perhaps on floor area utilised, then the result would almost certainly not have been the same.

The trend in modern manufacturing is for direct costs, and particularly direct labour costs, to reduce as a proportion of the total costs. This increases the importance of choosing the fairest method of apportionment.

Break even charts

In virtually all businesses, there is a close correlation between the level of turnover and the profit or loss. The managers know that, if invoiced sales reach a certain figure, the business will break even. If invoiced sales are above that figure the business will be in profit.

The break even point depends on the relationship between the fixed and the variable costs. If is often shown in the form of the following chart.

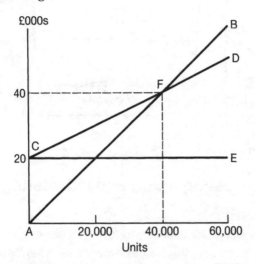

In the example, fixed costs (shown by line C–E) are £20 000. Variable costs are 50 pence per unit and the total costs (shown by line C–D) is the result of adding these to the fixed costs.

The revenue (shown by line A–B) is the result of sales at £1 per unit.

The break even point is 40 000 units sold at £1 each. This is equal to the total cost of £40 000 (£20 000 fixed and £20 000 variable). It is at point F where the lines cross. Profit or loss can also be read from the chart.

In practice, the relationships are rarely quite so straightforward, as some of the costs may be semi-variable.

Marginal costing and standard costing

Marginal costing
Marginal costing is a useful way of emphasising the marginal costs of production and services. This information is of great help in making pricing decisions.

If the selling price is less than the variable cost (direct cost), the loss will increase as more units are sold. Managers will only want to do this in very exceptional circumstances, such as a supermarket selling baked beans as a loss leader.

If the selling price is greater than the variable cost, then the margin will absorb part of the fixed costs. After a certain point profits will be made. Marginal costing explains why some goods and services are sold very cheaply. It explains, for example, why airline tickets are sometimes sold at low prices in the so-called bucket shops.

Once an airline is committed to making a flight, an extremely high part of the cost of that flight can properly be regarded as a fixed cost. The pilot's salary will be the same

whether the plane is empty or full. The variable cost is only
the complimentary meals and a few other items. It therefore
makes sense to make last minute sales of unsold seats at low
prices. So long as the selling price is greater than the
variable cost, then a contribution is made.

Standard costing
Standard costing involves the setting of targets, or
standards, for the different factors affecting costs. Variances
from the standard are then studied in detail.

For example:

Standard timber usage per unit of production	4.00 metres
Standard timber price	£2.00 per metre
Actual production	3 500 posts
Actual timber usage	14 140 metres
Actual cost of timber used	£27 714

Material Price Variance is   £566 favourable (2%)
(£28 280 less £27 714)

Material Usage Variance is   £280 adverse (1%)
([14 140 metres less 14 000 metres] × £2)

The material price variance happens because the standard
cost of the 14 140 metres used was £28 280 (at £2 per metre).
The actual cost was £27 714, a favourable variance of £566.
On the other hand 140 metres of timber too much was used,
resulting in an adverse material usage variance.

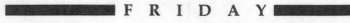

Summary

Costing is a big subject and there is only space to set out some of the basic principles. However, today we should have:

- Formed an understanding of the concept of costing
- Formed an understanding of the uses and value of costing
- Studied the principles of absorption costing
- Examined break even charts
- Answered the basic question 'what is marginal costing?'
- Answered the basic question 'what is standard costing?'

Tomorrow, we will finish our examination of finance with a look at budgets.

Budgets

We conclude the week by studying budgeting, probably the aspect of finance that has most impact on the time of non-financial managers.

We will look at:

- Budgeting in different types of organisations
- The profit budget
- The sales budget
- Revenue expenditure budgets
- The capital expenditure budget
- Cash and the Balance Sheet
- After the budget has been approved

Budgeting in different types of organisations

In very large organisations, hundreds of managers may be involved in the budgeting process, and the complete budget will probably be a very thick document. This would be true of say British Rail and, in the private sector, of companies such as Shell.

This involvement takes a lot of management time, but if the budgeting is done well it is likely to be time well spent. This is because the budget will probably be a realistic one, and because after approval the managers should feel committed to it.

When the budget has been approved, individual managers are responsible for their section of it. The responsibility is like a pyramid. At the base of the pyramid are the most junior managers supervising a comparatively small section, perhaps involving expenditure only. These junior managers should, however, have some knowledge of the overall budget and objectives.

In the middle may be more senior managers and divisional directors each with a wider area of responsibility for achieving the complete budget objectives. If everyone else meets their targets they will have an easy job.

Budgets should be designed to meet the needs of a particular organisation and its managers. For example, a 900-pupil school will probably have an expenditure budget of about £2 000 000. There will be little income and the budgeting emphasis will be on capital expenditure and revenue expenditure. The main aims will be informed choice and value for money.

The rest of today's work is devoted to the budget of a large company because this best illustrates the main principles. However, a smaller organisation should budget using the

same methods. There will be fewer managers involved, and less paper, but the same procedures should be followed.

On Sunday, we considered Julia Brown's book, and on Monday we considered John Brown's gardening business. Even their budgets follow the same principles. John Brown's van and motor mower constitute his capital expenditure budget. In their case the budgets will probably be on just one or two pieces of paper.

The profit budget

There are two basic approaches to budgeting in a large organisation, both having advantages and disadvantages.

- The so-called 'bottom up' method. Proposals are taken from the lower management levels. These are collated into an overall budget which may or may not be acceptable. If it is not, then top management calls for revisions.
- The so-called 'top down' method. Top management issues budget targets. Lower levels of management must then submit proposals that achieve these targets.

In practice, there is often less difference between the two methods than might be supposed. It is important that at some stage there is a full and frank exchange of views. Everyone should be encouraged to put forward any constructive point of view, and everyone should commit themselves to listening with an open mind. Needless to say, top management will, and should, have the final decisions.

All the budgets are important but in a commercial organisation the overall profit budget is likely to be considered the most important. A summarised six-month profit budget for a large organisation is given opposite. Please particularly note the following points:

Kingston Staplers Ltd. – Profit Budget for half year

	January	February	March	April	May	June	Total Half Year
	£000	£000	£000	£000	£000	£000	£000
Sales							
UK	1 500	1 400	1 450	1 700	1 600	1 800	9 450
Export	200	220	180	190	400	340	1 530
	1 700	1 620	1 630	1 890	2 000	2 140	10 980
Less cost of sales	1 020	970	990	1 150	1 230	1 320	6 680
Gross Profit	680	650	640	740	770	820	4 300
Overheads							
Sales Department	200	220	230	210	210	220	1 290
Finance Department	190	200	180	190	220	210	1 190
Administration Department	230	240	250	250	250	260	1 480
Total overheads	620	660	660	650	680	690	3 960
Net Profit/(Loss)	60	(10)	(20)	90	90	130	340

- Most budgets are for a year but this is not a requirement. They can be for six months or for any other useful period.
- This budget gives monthly figures, which is the most common division, but again this is not fixed. The divisions can be weekly, quarterly, or some other period.
- The figures are summarised in thousands of pounds. This is suitable for a summary budget of a large organisation. The budgets leading up to these summarised figures will be more detailed. January's budget for postage might, for example, be £2 850.
- As we will see, various subsidiary budgets and calculations feed figures through to this summary budget.

The sales budget

This should be in sufficient detail for the management to know from where the revenue will come. The figures will be broken down into different products and different sales regions. Each regional sales manager will have responsibility for a part of the sales budget. A section of the sales budget might look like the following:

Scottish Region Sales Budget

	Jan £	Feb £	March £
Product A	16 000	12 000	17 000
Product B	13 000	13 000	13 000
Product C	40 000	45 000	50 000
	69 000	70 000	80 000

Before the sales budget is done it would be normal for top management to issue budget assumptions concerning prices, competition, and other key matters.

The sales budget will be for orders taken. There will usually be a timing difference before orders become invoiced sales.

Revenue expenditure budgets

Still using the example of Kingston Staplers Ltd., the cost of sales will consist of direct wages, items bought for re-sale, raw materials and so on. The Sales, Finance, and Administration Departments will make up the overhead budget. In practice, this overhead budget is likely to be divided into three, with a different manager responsible for each section.

As with all the other budgets, each manager should submit a detailed budget for the section for which he is responsible. As with the sales budget, top management should give initial guidance on expected performance and policy assumptions. For example, a manager might be told to assume a company-wide average pay rise of 5% on April 1st.

The capital expenditure budget

This is extremely significant in some companies, less so in others. It will list all the planned capital expenditure showing the date when the expenditure will be made, and the date that the expenditure will be completed and the asset introduced to the business.

A sum for miscellaneous items is usually necessary. For example major projects might be listed separately and then £15 000 per month added for all projects individually less than £5 000.

Within the capital expenditure budget, timing is very important. Expenditure affects cash and interest straight away. Depreciation usually starts only on completion.

Cash and the Balance Sheet

When the profit budgets are complete, it is important that a cash budget is prepared. This is a Cash-Flow Forecast, which was examined in detail on Thursday. You might like to spend a few minutes referring back to this.

In practice, the profit budget and cash budget are linked and a chicken and egg problem has to be resolved. The profit budget cannot be completed until the interest figure is available. This in turn depends on the cash budget. The cash budget depends partly on the profit budget.

Dilemmas like this are quite common in budgeting. It is usual to put in an estimated figure for interest and then adjust everything later if necessary. This can be very time consuming, and budgeting is much simpler if the summarising is computerised. Several hours' work can be reduced to minutes and management is much freer to test budgets with useful 'what if' questions.

You will recall one of Monday's accounting rules which stated that every debit has a credit. It follows that every figure in the budgets has a forecastable consequence in a future Balance Sheet. It is normal to conclude the budgets by preparing a month-by-month forecast Balance Sheet and bankers are likely to ask for this. It may be that some aspect of the Balance Sheet is unacceptable and a partial re-budget is necessary.

In practice, top management is likely to review and alter some aspects of the budgets several times. Computers have made this easier.

After the budget has been approved

After the budget has been approved comes … quite possibly nothing at all. This is a pity but it does not mean that the budgeting exercise has been a waste of time. The participants will have thought logically about the organisation, its finances, and its future. Some of the detail will remain in their minds and influence their future actions.

Nevertheless, the budgets will be much more valuable if they are used in an active way. Regular performance reports should be issued by the accountants. These should be in the same format as the budgets, and should give comparable budget and actual figures. Variances should also be given.

All levels of management should regularly review these figures and explain the variances. Significant variances will pose the question of whether corrective action needs to be taken.

Finally, budgets do not necessarily have to be done just once a year. They may be updated, reviewed, or even scrapped and redone as circumstances dictate.

The week in summary

Finance affects the jobs of virtually all non-financial managers and during this week you should have significantly increased your knowledge of the subject. Many elements of finance have been examined and much ground has been covered.

The following summarises the subjects studied.

Profit Statements (Sunday)

- A simple example
- A trading company and a manufacturing company
- Further concepts
- A full example

Balance Sheets (Monday)

- What is a Balance Sheet?
- Accounting rules and a simple example
- Further concepts
- Test your knowledge

Published accounts (Tuesday)

- Availability of published accounts
- Profit and Loss Account and Balance Sheet
- Other items included in published accounts

Accounting ratios and investment decisions (Wednesday)

- Accounting ratios explained
- Understanding accounting ratios
- Investment decisions

Cash and the management of working capital (Thursday)

- Distinctions between cash and profit
- The Cash-Flow Forecast
- The management of working capital

Costing (Friday)

- The value and uses of costing
- Absorption costing
- Break-even charts
- Marginal costing and standard costing

Budgets (Saturday)

- The profit budget and associated budgets
- The capital expenditure budget
- Cash and the Balance Sheet
- After the budget has been approved

ABSORPTION COSTING   A costing system that involves all indirect costs being allocated to individual products or cost centres.

ACCRUALS   Costs for which value has been received, but which have not yet been entered into the books of account.

BAD DEBT   A debt that cannot be recovered and has to be written off.

BREAK EVEN POINT   The level of sales at which revenue equals the sum of fixed costs plus variable costs.

CAPITAL EXPENDITURE   Expenditure on items of a capital nature i.e. assets that will have a long term value.

CONSOLIDATED ACCOUNTS   The accounts of a holding company incorporating the accounts of all its subsidiary companies.

CONTINGENCIES   Costs that may be incurred in the future e.g. the cost of settling a pending legal action.

COST OF SALES   The cost of items sold (includes purchase price and manufacturing cost, but excludes overheads).

CREDITOR   Person to whom money is owed.

CURRENT ASSETS   Assets with a value available in the short term (usually taken to be less than a year).

CURRENT LIABILITIES   Liabilities which may have to be paid off in the short term (usually taken to be less than a year).

DEBTOR   Person from whom money is owed.

DEPRECIATION   The proportion of the cost of a fixed asset charged to the Profit and Loss account in a given period.

FIXED ASSETS   Assets that have a long term value and will generate revenue in the long term.

FIXED COSTS   Costs that do not vary according to the volume of activity e.g. business rates.

GROSS PROFIT   Profit after deducting direct costs of manufacture and purchase, but without deducting overheads.

NET PROFIT   Profit after deducting all costs including overheads. It is sometimes expressed as 'Net Profit Before Tax' and sometimes as 'Net Profit After Tax'.

PAYBACK   The period of time in which savings caused by capital expenditure equals the amount of the capital expenditure. No account is taken of interest.

PREPAYMENTS   Costs entered into the books of account for which the value has not yet been received.

STANDARD COSTS   Pre-set standard costs from which actual costs are measured.

STOCK SHRINKAGE   Reduction in stock caused by theft, evaporation, or similar causes.

STOCK TURN   The number of times that total stock is used (turned over) in the course of a year.

VARIABLE COSTS   Costs that vary according to the volume of activity e.g. direct wages.

WORKING CAPITAL   The amount by which current assets exceed current liabilities.